YOUR ECONOMIC FUTURE™

How Inflation Affects You

Terry Teague Meyer

ROSEN PUBLISHING®
New York

To Susan Thompson

Published in 2013 by The Rosen Publishing Group, Inc.
29 East 21st Street, New York, NY 10010

First Edition

Library of Congress Cataloging-in-Publication Data

Meyer, Terry Teague.
How inflation affects you/Terry Teague Meyer.—1st ed.
p. cm.—(Your economic future)
Includes bibliographical references and index.
ISBN 978-1-4488-8341-7 (library binding)
1. Inflation (Finance) I. Title.
HG229.M54 2013
332.024—dc23

2012018537

Manufactured in the United States of America

CPSIA Compliance Information: Batch #W13YA: For further information, contact Rosen Publishing, New York, New York, at 1-800-237-9932.

Contents

A rise in fuel prices has a ripple effect, increasing prices in many other areas of the economy.

Introduction

Sophia's parents worry a lot about money these days. They both have jobs, but they haven't gotten a raise in over a year and they feel like they are falling behind. When the rent increased, the family stopped eating out at restaurants. Sophia's mother says that the cost of eating at home is going up all the time, too. When Sophia had to have a cavity filled at the dentist's office, her parents were shocked that the cost of a filling was so much more than they remembered. Sophia had been saving up for a special pair of shoes, but she had to buy a cheaper pair to wear for the start of school. The ones she wanted had gotten too expensive. Her friend Caitlin's older sister had planned to start college this year but will have to begin part-time instead, due to the rising cost of tuition. Sophia's parents say they won't dip into her college savings no matter how tough their finances get. Sophia wonders if the amount saved, even if it goes untouched, will be enough to pay for college by the time she graduates from high school.

These family problems are caused by inflation, a gradual rise in prices over time that robs people of purchasing power (the ability to pay for what they need and want). In order to understand the impact of inflation, we need to answer a number of questions. What causes inflation? What are considered healthy or unhealthy rates of inflation and why? Why do costs in certain sectors (education, health care) rise faster than others (wages)? Does inflation always have a negative effect, or is there a way to benefit from it? What mechanisms drive inflation, and how does it affect government policy, national employment, and consumer behavior?

Understanding inflation and the issues surrounding it are part of gaining financial literacy so that you can effectively manage your money, even in dire periods of inflation (or deflation or recession or tight credit). Armed with this knowledge, you can come out on top, economically stable, secure, and confident.

Chapter 1

How Pricing Works

In terms of money, inflation means a rise in prices over time. Just as you inflate a balloon with air to make it bigger or add more helium to make it rise, inflation means the prices people pay for goods and services are inflating and rising ever higher. The annual rate of inflation rises and falls over time, but the trend is always upward.

Although consumers might not see rising prices as something good, the rate of inflation reflects the general health of the economy. Economists argue about the optimal rate of inflation for a healthy and growing economy, but an increase of between 2 to 3 percent each year is generally accepted to be ideal. Many factors affect the rate of inflation: consumer demand, government monetary policy, and international trade.

Supply and Demand

Underlying all pricing, especially price increases, is the economic law of supply and demand. There is a limited amount

Eager customers are willing to stand in line to buy the latest products. Such high demand fuels inflation.

of goods (things you buy) and services (things you pay others to do for you) available. Think about people camping out in line for tickets to a popular concert or the newest smartphone or game console. Here, the number of people wanting a limited number of tickets or new products is greater than the supply available. Consequently, people may be willing to stand in line for hours or pay much more for a concert ticket or above list price for the latest consumer electronic gadget. In times of natural disaster, people have been charged unreasonable prices for necessities like ice and water, which tend to be in very short supply.

Hard Choices

Inflation affects all of us as prices rise for necessities like food, water, electricity, housing, fuel to heat and cool our homes, gas to transport us, and the various household and personal products we need. If salaries rise at the same rate of inflation, people can keep pace with rising prices for the goods and services they desire. However, salaries tend to lag behind price increases, forcing families and individuals to make hard budget choices. For example, if the rent increases, a family might have to give up entertainment or eating out. When the cost of electricity or fuel oil goes up, consumers may have to adjust the thermostat to save on heat and electricity or put off buying nonessential goods like new clothes. They may have to make do by keeping the old family car on the road for another year or two; buying secondhand clothes, books, or furniture; or buying generic instead of name-brand foods at the supermarket.

These are extreme examples, but they illustrate the force of supply and demand. When people really need and want certain goods and services, they are willing to pay more for them than in the past. When a lot of people want the same product or service, demand outstrips supply and prices rise. This is because producers and sellers, seeking higher profits, raise prices as soon as they realize their products are now worth more.

Let's use a fictional scenario to illustrate how inflation is related to supply and demand. Matt is a computer whiz who helps family members solve their computer problems and create personal Web sites. In order to earn money, he goes into business using his computer and Web expertise. At first, he is happy to charge a very small amount ($5 an hour), since he is earning money for what he used to do for free. However, as word gets around among his parents' friends, he soon has more customers than he has time for and realizes that his services are more valuable than he realized. He begins charging $10 an hour and finds that he still has all the customers he can handle.

But when Matt begins charging $15 an hour, he discovers that fewer people want his services at this price. Besides that, his neighbor Emily has started

When crop failures caused by weather or plant disease decrease the food supply, prices go up.

distributing fliers for her competing computer service, and she's charging only $11 an hour. Matt's higher fees have slowed the demand for his once in-demand services. People might decide to put off designing a Web site or try to do it themselves if the price seems too high. Competition from Emily is also decreasing demand for Matt's service. He will have to consider adjusting his price or risk driving away even more customers.

Types of Inflation

There are two types of inflation. Cost-push inflation occurs when the price of raw materials or labor forces the producer to increase the price it charges for goods and services. If a natural disaster like a hard freeze or a plant disease dramatically reduces the supply of apples, for example, producers of apple sauce, apple juice, and other apple products would likely raise prices to cover the cost of finding new sources of a scarce product. If skilled workers are in short supply and employers must pay more to attract them, businesses will pass the increased cost along to consumers when pricing their products.

Cost-push inflation has a cumulative effect. Like a snowball growing larger, as the price of one product increases, that higher cost will lead to other price increases throughout the economy. Crude oil provides a good example of this phenomenon. A rise in the price of crude oil affects many other products and services. Higher-priced gasoline affects almost everything else in the economy because it increases the cost of transporting goods. Retailers must pay more to get products into their stores. Florists, newspapers, pizza makers, and others must pay more to make home deliveries. Cities must adjust to the higher cost of running subways and trains and fueling police cars, fire engines, and school and city buses. In addition, petroleum is the basis of a multitude of plastics and chemicals found in products that we use daily. The increased cost of these products and their packaging will also be passed along to consumers. Higher costs in so many areas at once make life particularly difficult for people who make minimum wage or have a fixed income, such as Social Security. As prices rise for many necessities, people may have to put off paying bills or cut back on necessities like food and medicine.

The second form of inflation is demand-pull. When consumers have more money, they tend to spend it. They will likely pay for more nonessential goods and services like clothing, electronics, and vacations. Or they may purchase big-ticket items like new cars and appliances that they have been putting off buying. The increased demand for goods and services pulls the prices up. You can see demand-pull at work in auction situations like eBay and television shopping networks. Seeing that other people want the same product they do, a sort of consumer competition erupts, and the demand pulls the price up.

Demand-pull inflation makes it easier to understand how inflation relates to the health of the economy. When consumers have more cash on hand and spend it, they create increased demand for products and services. The economy is then said to be expanding or heating up. Businesses are encouraged to expand, buy new equipment and machines, hire additional employees, pay higher salaries, or offer workers additional paid work hours. However, if the expanding

Fast-food restaurants compete for customers by keeping prices low. Special prices entice consumers to buy more and keep coming back.

economy causes prices to rise too much, it leads to economic instability. People are reluctant to make financial decisions because they are unsure what prices will be in the future.

Explaining Inflation Inequality

The impact of supply and demand doesn't explain all price fluctuations. The rate of inflation varies from one area to another, raising a number of questions. Why do fast-food meals remain relatively cheap, while the cost of food in a sit-down restaurant or movie theater keeps going up? Why do wages tend to lag behind rising prices, while the cost of health care and college tuition outpace the overall rate of inflation?

These questions are not easy to answer. In his book *Why Popcorn Costs So Much at the Movies and Other Pricing Puzzles*, business professor Richard McKenzie discusses how products are priced so that businesses can maximize profits. For example, the price of a new smartphone is high when it first comes out because some people are willing to pay a high price to be the first to get it. When the first wave of sales drops, the price will drop, too. The new lower price will attract additional customers, and the manufacturer still enjoys a healthy profit from the increased numbers of sales.

Competition is also important in determining price. Competition is fierce among fast-food restaurants, which need a large number of customers to make a profit. They offer specials and "super-sizing" to keep customers coming back. And you may have noticed that although the large combination meals are a "bargain," they also encourage people to buy (and possibly eat) more than they would if they bought only the individual items that they truly desired.

Technology affects pricing as well. The higher cost of health care covers tests, procedures, and equipment unavailable in the past. The cost of developing and manufacturing health care innovations has raised the price of health care in general. On the other hand, technology has helped reduce the cost of manufacturing by making it more efficient and inexpensive (for example, using robots and advanced machines, rather than human labor to build a machine). Once a new product has been developed, other companies can copy it and make their own versions, often using cheaper foreign labor. This helps explain why electronics and household

The high rate of inflation for college tuition is creating a crisis in education.

gadgets remain relatively inexpensive. Technological advances also help explain why salaries tend to lag behind the rate of inflation. These advances enable manufacturers to allow more work to be done by machines or foreign workers who can carry out data entry, customer service, and other tasks through computer networking.

College costs have increased not only because more Americans are attending college but also because colleges and universities compete for the best students and are constantly upgrading their campuses and facilities to attract these students. At the same time, states have reduced funding for higher education and passed the costs along in the form of higher tuition and fees. Students and their families are now bearing more direct costs previously covered by taxpayers.

Chapter 2

Monetary Policy

Consumer spending affecting supply and demand is not the only force causing changes in the rate of inflation. Our government's monetary policies also play an important part. Monetary policy refers to the government's role in determining how much money is circulating in the economy.

We know that money is valuable—it enables us to buy goods and services. But what gives paper money its value? In the past, the American dollar was backed by gold. People could point to the government's stores of gold and say that each dollar was equal to a certain amount of that gold. Dollars could even be redeemed for its equivalent in gold. However, that has not been the case in quite some time. In 1971, President Richard Nixon took the final step in abandoning the gold standard when he announced that the United States would no longer redeem currency for gold.

Since then, the U.S. dollar, like the currency of most other countries, is "fiat money," issued by the government without legal restraints. What gives the dollar value is the full faith and credit of the U.S. government. People's belief in the strength of the American economy causes them to accept the worth of the dollar. The worth of the dollar is accepted not only in the United States but also around the world.

Gold held by the U.S. government is far less than the value of dollars in the American economy.

As long as the value of the dollar was tied to a commodity such as gold, the supply of money could not increase rapidly, as it was limited by the amount of gold to back it up. Freed from the gold standard, however, the money supply could now be controlled by the government in an effort to stimulate or slow down the economy as a whole. What is meant by the term "money supply"? The money supply is more than the dollar bills and coins in circulation. Deposits held by the public in banks and other depository institutions (like thrift funds and credit unions) are also included.

Hyperinflation

Since the government has the ability to print more money and increase the money supply, what prevents it from just printing more and more? In wartime, governments have indeed financed war efforts by simply increasing the money supply. However, doing so creates problems. Economists recognize that increasing the money supply is a major cause of inflation. A larger supply of money makes each dollar worth less.

There are a number of twentieth-century examples of countries printing so much money that the currency lost nearly all of its value. The most dramatic examples of a rapid, continuing rise in the rate of inflation (called hyperinflation) are Weimar Germany; post–World War II Hungary, Greece, and Taiwan; early 1990s Yugoslavia; and present-day Zimbabwe. During Germany's hyperinflationary period of 1920–1923, the rate of inflation rose almost 30,000 percent each month, and people took to burning currency to heat their homes. Zimbabwe began printing bills of larger and larger denominations, including a $100 billion bill in 2008. The $100 trillion bill printed just six months later was said to be worth around US$30.

It's easy to see how hyperinflation (a rate of inflation of 50 percent or more each month) would cause uncertainty and instability in a country. People would not want to save money only to see its value quickly decrease. Instead of working to earn a salary that is worth less every day, they would want to acquire goods as fast as possible before prices rose even more and the value of their wages eroded further. Manufacturers would not know how to price their wares to adjust for inflation while also trying to figure out

The depreciation in the value of money in post-WWI Germany made paper notes so worthless that children used them as toy building blocks.

how to cover expenses and make a profit. Logically, people would resort to bartering (exchanging goods and services without using money).

The Business Cycle

The U.S. government actively participates in the economy, partly through the U.S. Federal Reserve System, often called the Fed. This system of banks and policy makers was established in 1913 in an effort to curb the extreme economic fluctuations that had troubled the country for many years. Today, as when it was first established, the Fed's main purpose is to stabilize the American economy. It aims to protect the purchasing power of the U.S. dollar by controlling inflation while promoting a robust economy and healthy employment levels. To do so, the Fed tries to balance the flow of money and credit with the needs of the economy. The Fed controls the amount of money available to banks and other financial institutions. These, in turn, invest or loan money to businesses and individuals.

In order to make decisions about monetary policy, economists at the Fed must constantly analyze economic data like prices and employment figures. Monetary policy is just one tool used to influence the economy—to keep it growing at a healthy rate, but not so fast that it causes inflation to rise too much or too fast. Economic growth tends to go in cycles, often referred to as the business cycle. It is characterized by a movement from expansion to peak to recession to trough to recovery, and back to expansion. When the economy is expanding, employment, spending, and prices rise. Demand for products and services makes businesses want to improve

Stagflation and the Misery Index

In most cases, when the economy is expanding and inflation is rising, more people are working. However, that is not always the case. "Stagflation" describes a situation in which both the rate of inflation and the rate of unemployment are high at the same time. During the period from 1973 to 1981, Americans considered the inflation-driven high cost of living the major problem facing the country. At the same time, a recession, also caused by high rates of inflation, was keeping unemployment rates high as well. The government responded to this situation by taking a more active role in economic oversight through the Fed.

Economist Arthur Okun created the "misery index" during the 1960s to help determine how the average citizen is doing economically. The misery index is the sum of the rate of inflation and unemployment. The higher the index, the worse people are doing financially. During 2009, a period of recession caused the inflation rate to be negative, but the rising rate of unemployment meant that the misery index just kept going up. In January 2009, there was a very low rate of inflation (.03 percent) and unemployment was 7.8 percent, resulting in a misery index of 7.83. In a period of stagflation like that experienced in the 1970s, the high rate of inflation would be stacked on the high rate of unemployment to create a double-digit misery index and a bleak snapshot of a truly miserable economy.

and expand their facilities and hire more workers. With an increased need for labor, employees can work more hours or ask for bigger salaries, giving them more money to spend, thus fueling the economy still more.

However, if inflation causes prices to rise too much or too fast, it can bring about uncertainty. Consumers have trouble making financial decisions. Would it be better to buy a new car now because the price will likely go up in the near future? Aware that high inflation is eroding their savings and the purchasing power of their paychecks, consumers may be reluctant to spend. Therefore, after a period of expansion (growth), the economy may stop growing and enter a period of recession, which is the opposite of expansion. In a recession, the rate of inflation may actually be negative. In this case, it is called deflation. That might sound good, but falling prices are usually accompanied by the loss of jobs. Like a balloon losing air, the economy is going flat. The role of the Fed is to

When the economy is expanding, more job opportunities become available.

control the money supply in an effort to offset and smooth out the steep ups and downs of the economic cycle.

Interest Rates

The Fed sets the interest rates charged to financial institutions and sets requirements on the amount of money depository institutions must keep in reserve. The Fed's discount rate of interest to banks is important. This is because lower interest rates encourage borrowing and thus economic expansion, while higher rates are designed to do the opposite. The Fed's decisions have little direct, immediate effect on consumer spending, but its decisions have a long-term impact on inflation.

Interest rates have a huge impact on the economy, since most business and individual transactions are based on credit. Rather than pay for raw materials or equipment with available funds, businesses borrow money both to get started and continue growing. Americans increasingly make purchases large and small with credit cards, and they use long-term financing for big-ticket items like appliances, computers, and cars. When interest rates are low, the cost of borrowing is minimal, so people are likely to borrow and spend more. When interest rates are high, the cost of borrowing adds substantially to what is being purchased and therefore discourages spending.

The Fed's Track Record

How successful has the Fed been in maintaining the purchasing power of the dollar? According to investment banker

When buying on credit, consumers should consider the extra cost in interest and fees accrued over the time it takes to pay off the purchase.

James Rickards, the dollar has lost 95 percent of its value since the creation of the Fed in 1913—not a good track record. At the same time, however, wages have increased by a factor of twenty, offsetting the loss of purchasing power.

While critical of the Fed's effectiveness in maintaining the value of the dollar, Rickards notes that certain influences on the economy simply can't be controlled. One of the most important of these is the confidence of individuals in their own economic prospects and the general confidence of consumers as a group. Inflation impacts consumer confidence, even when the rate of inflation is relatively low. People fear that they can't keep up with prices, that they are never going to get ahead, and that they are losing ground to others. As we have seen, varying rates of inflation and varying rates of interest create different economic winners and losers. Try as it might to keep the economy at a "Goldilocks point" that is neither too hot nor too cold, the Fed can't ensure prosperity for all Americans.

Instead, the government's efforts to stabilize the economy often have unintended consequences. Following a drastic slowdown in the economy in early 2000, the Fed cut interest rates sharply to spur growth. It continued to keep interest rates low throughout the decade in an effort to encourage businesses to invest. However, corporations failed to take advantage of the low rates. Instead, individuals rushed to take advantage of lower rates to buy houses. The price of real estate rose rapidly because of the increased demand—only to drop sharply later with disastrous results, leading to the "Great Recession" of 2007–2009. Although the United States has considerable political and economic influence around the world, the prices we pay for things often depend on conditions outside our borders, which our government can't control.

Chapter 3

Inflation and Globalization

Look at the labels in the clothing you wear or the origin of the products you use every day, and you will likely find something made somewhere outside the United States. While we are constantly importing foreign goods into the United States, American farmers and manufacturers export their products to people worldwide. We cannot talk about the American economy without considering its trading partners, as we are increasingly tied economically to other countries.

The Exchange Rate

Every day, business leaders and world travelers can check financial Web sites or the business sections of newspapers to find out the current value of the dollar relative to the currencies of other countries. Due to ever-changing economic conditions of nations worldwide, the value of a

Most of the products Americans buy today are made outside the United States. China is a major supplier of these consumer goods.

dollar compared to the euro, for example, can change daily. Consequently, a family that travels to Europe on vacation and charges purchases might find that the cost of what they thought they were paying in dollars has changed by the time they get a credit card bill a few weeks later.

On a larger scale, the rate of exchange affects imports and exports tremendously. When the value of the dollar is relatively high (known as a strong dollar) against another currency, the cost of American exports rises abroad. Consequently, Americans have more difficulty selling their goods in other countries because they are more expensive in terms of the importing country's currency. On the other

The relative value of the U.S. dollar to other currencies has a huge impact on the price of American imports and exports.

hand, with a strong dollar, Americans can buy foreign goods at lower prices. Yet when the value of the dollar is lower than that of another currency, American exporters benefit and American consumers have to pay more for imported goods.

Layoffs and Outsourcing U.S. Jobs

While Americans enjoy getting imported goods at reasonable prices, the effect of a strong dollar on exports can have a negative effect on the American economy in general. If American companies cannot sell their goods overseas, workers at home are likely to lose jobs. Without paychecks, these workers spend less, the economy slows, and further rounds of layoffs become likely, as do further decreases in consumer spending. A negative economic cycle has begun.

Labor costs overseas are another factor in keeping down the cost of imported goods. The United States has a very high standard of living, and American workers demand higher wages in order to maintain that standard of living. Our economy is fueled in part by consumer demand for inexpensive products, many of them grown, produced, or manufactured in developing countries where salary expectations are very low. Comparing American salaries with those in developing countries is a bit like comparing apples and oranges. The China Briefing daily news service reported in January 2011 that the combined salary and government benefits for a typical Chinese worker totaled around $2,250 a year. This was compared to an annual total of $1,152 for a Vietnamese worker and $943 for an Indian. Each of these countries is experiencing rapid economic development, in part because low

China's Unfair Advantage?

China has been criticized in recent years for keeping the value of its currency, the renminbi (also known as the yuan), artificially low in relation to the dollar. American purchases of Chinese products at low prices provide manufacturing jobs for more Chinese workers instead of Americans. In turn, Chinese consumers are less likely to buy higher-priced American goods, hurting American manufacturers and their employees.

wages have resulted in low prices for the nations' manufactured goods. These low prices have created huge worldwide demand and stimulated economic growth.

In an effort to keep production costs down and compete in global markets, American companies have moved factories to countries

The loss of American jobs to lower-paid workers overseas affects whole communities and states.

where labor is cheap. This practice is known as outsourcing. This trend has left American workers, particularly those in manufacturing jobs, facing unemployment and the need for additional career training and education to enable them to find work in new fields. Technology is also helping American businesses operate more efficiently and increase productivity in order to remain competitive. Unfortunately, improved technology often means workers lose jobs to machines. In addition, computer networking has made it possible to move data entry work and customer service centers to other countries, resulting in still more losses of American jobs.

Some manufacturing jobs that were once outsourced overseas are being restored to American workers. These American workers are assembling combination padlocks for Master Lock of Milwaukee, Wisconsin, a company that has recently insourced its labor.

It is understandable for shoppers to look for bargains—either for the satisfaction of getting the best deal or out of necessity. However, buying foreign-made goods has had a profoundly negative impact on American unemployment. As American manufacturing jobs shift to other countries, the resulting unemployment has done great damage to American families and the towns and communities in which they live. Consider that the closing of a major center of employment, such as a factory, mill, or distribution center, in a small town creates a ripple effect, leading to the loss of income among stores and restaurants in the area. As people move away to seek employment, the community tax base erodes, and schools and local governments suffer.

Jobs lost overseas may not be lost forever, however. In early 2012, National Public Radio (NPR) reported on a trend toward reclaiming jobs for Americans. President Barack Obama called it "insourcing" (the opposite of "outsourcing"). One report talked about Master Lock moving manufacturing jobs back to Milwaukee, Wisconsin. The company was responding to rising labor costs in China, rising productivity at home, and rising fuel costs to ship goods across the Pacific Ocean. Another company, Hiawatha Rubber, cited the poor quality of Chinese-made products as a reason for bringing jobs back to America. The trend was characterized as still being a "trickle" in comparison to the "tidal wave" of jobs leaving the United States, but it's still a positive trend.

True or False?

All inflation is bad.

FALSE Inflation can stimulate the economy and sometimes provides extra money for companies, as well as their employees. When companies have extra money, they can share their profits with workers. They can also use that money to develop better products.

During inflationary periods, prices for only some goods and services are rising.

TRUE Inflation might mean that some products and services have increased in price, while prices for other products and services remain the same or even decrease. A period of inflation features price increases for a large number of—but not necessarily all—popular goods and services over an extended period of time.

Higher inflation means higher wages.

FALSE Just because the economy is experiencing inflation does not mean that workers will receive higher wages to keep up with that inflation. Sometimes, company owners can't afford to increase the wages of their workers. During an inflationary period, company owners often have to pay higher prices for the materials and services that they have to buy in order to keep their companies in business. This leaves them with less money with which to offer raises to their employees.

Chapter 4

Inflation and the Local Scene

Unlike the federal government, states and municipalities such as towns, cities, and counties cannot control the flow of money—primarily tax dollars—that comes in to fund and support their operations and services. Consequently, these public entities must deal with severe budget problems in the face of rising prices and falling revenues. When people earn less, they pay less in taxes. When they spend less because they are earning less, companies make less money, and they, too, pay less in taxes. Lower tax revenue means less funds to pay for city or state programs and services.

We often take the basic services provided by local government entities for granted. State and local governments build and maintain parks and schools, the streets we drive on, the bridges and tunnels we cross, the water and sewer lines connected to our homes, and so much more. Municipalities must employ a large number of workers such as police, sanitation workers, inspectors, groundskeepers, firefighters,

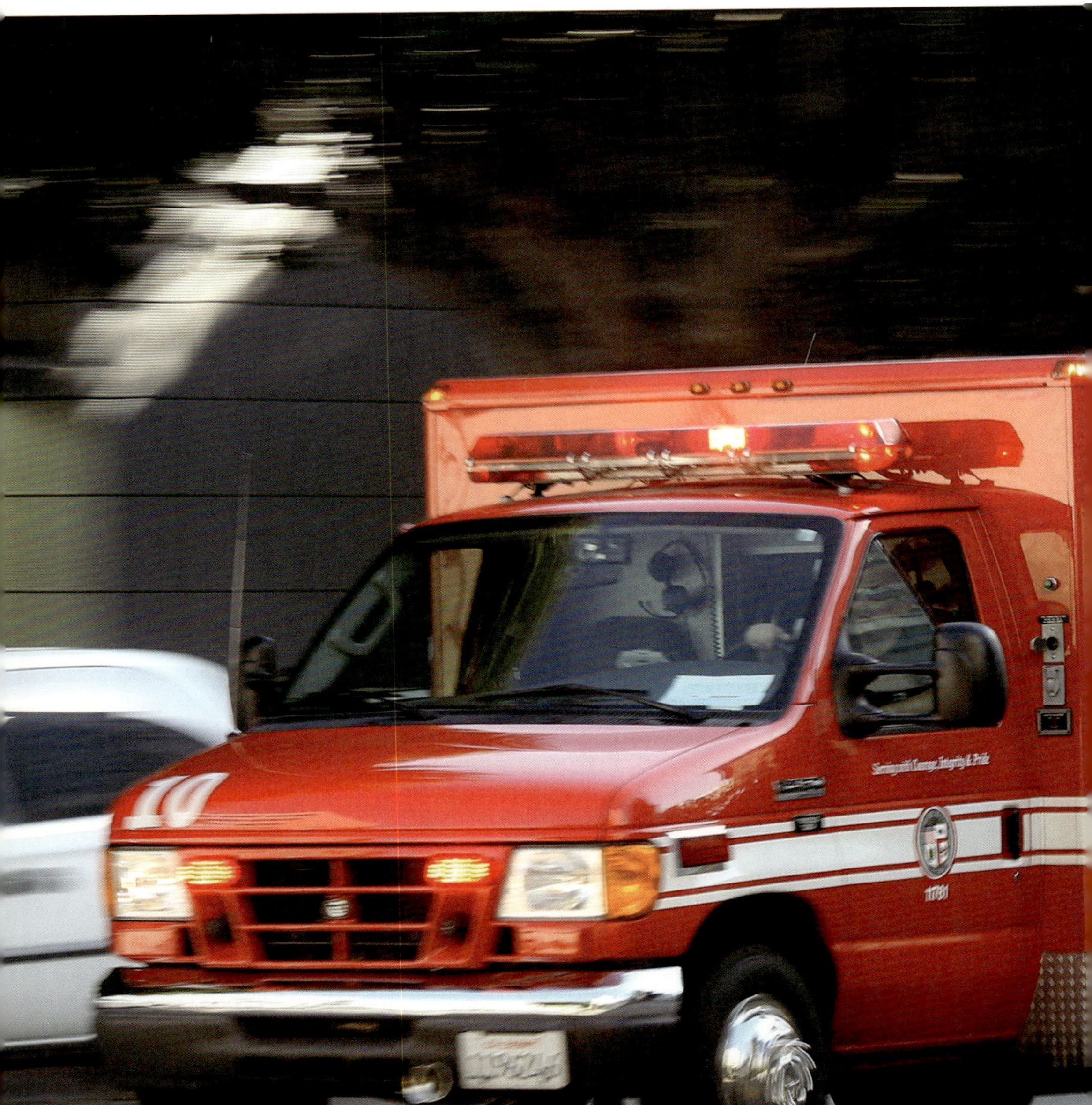

Inflation and loss of tax revenue put pressure on municipalities to maintain essential services, like emergency medical services, police officers, firefighters, and public transportation.

and the administrators and office workers needed to support these workers and many others. Municipalities are funded by taxes (primarily property taxes), sale of municipal bonds, and by various licensing and user fees. As inflation puts pressure on municipalities to cover rising costs, its effect on municipal funding is complex.

Property Taxes

Property taxes are based on the value of a piece of real estate, such as a home, office, commercial building, or even undeveloped land. The value attached to the property can be calculated in a number of ways, but it is usually figured as a certain amount for each increment of value. For example, let's say that a school district votes to charge a dollar of tax for each $100 of the value of a property. In this situation, a house worth

$200,000 would be taxed $2,000 for the year. That doesn't sound like much, but it would represent only the amount of taxes charged for the school district. The same property owner would be subject to taxes from other local entities, such as the town, the county, the flood control district, the hospital district, and others, depending on the organization of the local government. All of these taxes add up quickly, making property taxes a major expense for homeowners. Renters also pay these taxes in the form of increased rental charges. Businesses are likely to pass the cost of rising taxes along to their customers in one way or another.

In a period of rapidly rising housing costs, municipalities would seem to benefit because they are bringing in more money in taxes. If a house assessed (valued) at $200,000 one

Renewal of run-down neighborhoods can be good for some affluent residents and property owners, but it can place extreme financial pressure on less well-off neighbors.

year was valued at $300,000 two years later, the taxing entities would take in 50 percent more in taxes. Older neighborhoods (often in inner-city areas) with low property values and dilapidated buildings are said to become "gentrified" when new owners purchase and improve, rebuild, and replace previously undervalued homes and businesses. Property values rise, and property taxes rise with them. The area may become gentrified because of location or because property could be bought cheaply. For the newcomers, it's a good situation, but existing businesses and homeowners may suffer. Higher property values mean higher taxes, which those on fixed incomes may be unable to pay. Retirees and families struggling to get by might lose their homes.

In 1978, in response to rising taxes due to high property values, California taxpayers fought back, passing what is known as Proposition 13. Proposition 13 limited the total amount of property taxes to 1 percent of the value of the property and increases due to inflation to no more than 2 percent a year. Long after its passage, the results of Proposition 13 illustrate the disastrous effects of keeping taxes low in the face of rising inflation. Municipal costs have risen in California, while the ability to raise property taxes has been limited. The lower taxes have meant the state of California, as well as its cities and communities, have had to cut costs drastically. Local governments have raised fees and sales taxes to make up for budget shortfalls. These revenue sources often have the greatest impact on lower-income families. Since Proposition 13 was enacted, the national ranking of California schools, dependent for their funding on property taxes, has slipped from among the top of the list of states to near the bottom.

Falling Bond Values and Increasing Fees

Inflation affects municipal bonds, another source of funding for schools and municipalities, in a different way. Bonds are fixed-income financial assets, basically IOUs that promise the buyer a specified set of payments. The issuer (the borrower) promises to pay back the money invested over time, plus interest. The interest rate on the bond is usually fixed; no matter what happens to market interest rates after it is purchased, the interest rate on the bond won't change.

Not surprisingly, the value of bonds falls when inflation rises. If you invested in a bond that is supposed to pay back your investment plus interest over a period of ten years, a high rate of inflation would lessen the value of your investment during that time. In addition, the greater the uncertainty about whether the promised payments will be made (the risk that the issuer will fail to pay back the IOU), the lower the value of the bond. Municipal bonds are attractive to many investors because they are traditionally free of federal taxes, but they become less attractive in a period of high inflation.

A municipality suffering budget difficulties because of high inflation might increase fees in an attempt to generate another stream of income. Fees could come in the form of higher costs for parking on city streets, reserving picnic areas in city parks, licenses for pets, and required licenses and building inspections. Although such fees are paid by direct users of the service, they are usually passed along by businesses to their customers in the form of higher prices. Often, a service formerly covered by taxes and free of additional user

Municipalities may establish or increase user fees to offset inflation or falling tax revenues.

fees becomes yet another personal expense for individuals and families in an inflationary period. On the other hand, cities and schools may decide to deal with smaller budgets by reducing services—increasing class size in schools, being slower to fill street potholes or clear the streets of snow, and cutting bus service, for example. The effect of all this is the same for families and individuals—a reduction in quality of life, making people long for the "good ol' days."

When the Bubble Bursts

Beginning in 2006, the collapse of the housing bubble was a disaster for many communities, cities, and entire states. During this period of rising unemployment, many people were unable to make mortgage payments. Although the price of real estate dropped quickly—particularly in areas where it had risen based on

A Real Estate Bubble

In order to buy something as expensive as a piece of property, almost everyone must take out a large loan, called a mortgage. The mortgage will be paid back over a very long time, often fifteen to thirty years. The owner typically pays a substantial down payment and makes monthly payments at a rate of interest that may stay the same or may change (fixed rate or variable rate). During the early years, the monthly mortgage payments basically go to pay the interest costs on the loan, but the homeowner is said to be building up equity in the property. The owner who fails to make payments on the mortgage risks losing the property, which is not actually owned by him or her until the mortgage is paid off.

In a real estate bubble, people see the cost of housing going up very quickly and want to buy something before prices go up further. Some of these purchasers are treating the home as an investment, hoping to buy low and sell high. This buying frenzy creates a high demand and pushes housing costs up even more quickly. At the same time, builders jump in to meet the increased demand for housing, but they must borrow to finance the cost of construction materials and labor.

In the early 2000s, banks and other lenders, eager to profit from the demand for mortgages, offered loans to people who really didn't have the means to repay them. They also offered mortgages with variable rates. Once interest rates rose in response to rising inflation, these mortgage holders could no longer afford their monthly payments, which had increased sharply with the interest rate hike. Borrowers were unable to keep up on their mortgage payments and lost their homes to foreclosure, increasing the supply of available housing and driving down the cost.

The buying frenzy halted, and demand plummeted as the market was glutted with unsold houses. Whole neighborhoods under construction could not be completed, as the builders couldn't finance more construction by selling what they had already built. Houses in the neighborhood of foreclosed homes lost value as well. Homeowners who could make their mortgage payments felt cheated, finding themselves with a mortgage in which they owed tens of thousands of dollars more than the current value of their property. This unique situation, in which a homeowner owes more on a house loan than the home is actually worth, is known as an "underwater mortgage."

false expectations of ever-increasing home values—the cost of other basics like food, transportation, health, and education did not fall. In order to stay in homes that were no longer worth the value of the mortgage, homeowners were forced to pay a great deal of their income toward housing. In effect, what they thought was an asset (their real estate) had become a liability.

Home foreclosures had a dramatic effect on local communities. In many areas, the tax base of affected communities—the value of the properties on which their taxes are assessed—was drastically reduced. Take our previous example of a house worth $200,000. Now consider it losing value and becoming worth only $150,000. All the government entities relying on property taxes would feel the pain of lost revenue due to lower home values and assessments. In addition, as people moved out of foreclosed homes, leaving many houses and whole neighborhoods abandoned, the lack of maintenance and the threat of vandalism would likely mean increased costs for the local government. With fewer occupants to maintain homes and yards and watch out for their neighbors comes a greater possibility of fire, vandalism, and criminal activity, all of which must be combatted by local authorities and services.

Foreclosed and vacant houses cause problems for the neighbors and the larger community.

The end of a real estate bubble could mean problems for municipal bond sales as well. Projects such as the building of bridges and schools or the expansion of water and sewer facilities might come to a halt as community growth becomes community stagnation. As a result, a municipality's future bonds might have to be sold for less money. If a municipality's finances were troubled, its bond rating might be downgraded, signaling that the municipality is at an elevated risk of failing to repay its bondholders.

The city of Stockton, California, provides an example of what can happen in an area caught between rising costs and falling property values. As reported in the *New York Times* in March 2012, Stockton, a city of three hundred thousand, was the largest city in the United States on the brink of declaring bankruptcy. With one hundred fewer police officers than four years before, the city was seeing a record number of murders. Building projects begun in the boom years of the previous decade became a drain on the city budget when the tax base shrank. In addition to laying off employees, the city suspended $2 million in debt payments for 2012.

Alan Farnham of ABC News reported in September 2011 on Vallejo, another California city that declared bankruptcy in 2008. Unable to pay its bills, the city cut its police department in half and saw crime soar. Neighborhood watch programs, manned by residents, tried to keep criminals out of residential areas. Harrisburg, the capital of Pennsylvania; Boise County, Idaho; Jefferson County, Alabama; and the small city of Central Falls, Rhode Island, have all found themselves in similar situations due to the financial collapse of local governments.

According to ABC News, the decline of Central Falls began decades ago as textile manufacturers moved plants

As cities and communities in financial difficulty cut services, they become less attractive to investors and potential home buyers. This Central Falls, Rhode Island, library has been closed indefinitely due to budget cuts, decreasing the community's quality of life.

overseas. Eventually, 1,400 jobs were lost and the town was impoverished. Before declaring bankruptcy, the town closed the library and a community center and experienced a tremendous increase in crime. Because Jefferson County can't afford to repair its aging, unsafe bridges, school buses are forced to drive around them. This inconvenience is costly, adding over 1,700 miles (2,736 kilometers) a year to bus routes and $2.5 million in added fuel costs.

Problems in Vallejo and Central Falls resulted from the loss of major employers in the area. Harrisburg, Jefferson County, and Boise County suffered from disasters in municipal finance. Residents in all these areas are facing a bleak future. Homeowners who have lost jobs may default on their mortgages and lose their homes. They cannot easily sell their property and look for jobs somewhere else. The value of their homes has dwindled, so they are unlikely to sell them for the value of their mortgage. Even those families who are financially secure now find themselves living in communities experiencing high crime rates and slashed public services and amenities.

Imagine for a moment how the collapse of an inflationary real estate bubble might impact your community. Prices for necessities like fuel and health care continue to rise, perhaps at a rate of inflation greater than the national cost of living index. Like a family having to cut back on nonessential spending in order to pay bills, the town would have to limit services. It would cut back on street cleaning and garbage pickup, and eliminate shelters for the homeless, affordable health clinics, and afterschool programs for at-risk youths. School districts might slash library budgets, making do with old and outdated books and computers, while also eliminating athletic programs and extracurricular clubs and activities.

It is very difficult for bankrupt municipalities to recover, since they have little to attract new businesses and residents. Having defaulted on debt, they will have difficulty selling bonds in the future. Their bond rating will be downgraded, and they will likely have to offer higher interest rates to attract bondholders in the future. Financial help might come from the state or federal government. However, the trend is for states to reduce funding and leave local school districts and municipalities to manage for themselves as best they can.

Chapter 5

Inflation and Your Finances

Economists and consumers would all like to see the American economy expanding steadily in such a way that employment stays high and prices don't rise too fast. However, as we have seen, there are many factors influencing the rate of inflation. The Fed can control interest rates, but it can control neither consumer confidence in the future nor the response of foreign investors to fluctuating interest rates. It is obvious from the attention that Wall Street has paid to the recent debt problems of the European Economic Community (EEC) that international buying, selling, and lending link our financial future to that of other countries. Experts in economics and finance attempt to make the best of price fluctuations, but their efforts often have unintended consequences, particularly for the general public.

We have seen that there are winners and losers in inflationary and deflationary periods. Mortgage holders benefit from higher inflation, paying off their loans with cheaper dollars over the years. At the same time, bondholders see their investments shrink over time, and savers lose much of the value of their money. In times of high inflation, consumers may think it wise to invest in housing or consumer goods before prices rise still further. However, by doing so, they may incur too much debt or fail to save enough to provide a cushion to protect them in the event of financial disaster, such as a major illness or loss of employment.

The Value of Good Advice and Diversification

The best plan for financial growth and security includes diversity of investments. Individuals and families should not invest all their money in one area—be it a savings account, a house, or bonds. All investments carry risk—high inflation can eat up savings, falling prices can reduce the value

Consumers should seek investment and financial planning advice from a reputable, trusted, and credentialed professional.

of a home. For this reason, it is best to adopt a mix of savings and investment strategies. Investments with higher risk also tend to have higher returns, while safer, conservative investments provide lower returns.

Because of the complexity of the financial world, it is best to do research and find a reputable investment counselor to help develop a plan. The investment adviser will work to find a balance of risk and growth that best suits the investor's needs. The plan will have to be reviewed and revised over time as financial needs and conditions change. The financial goals of a young person with substantial college debt or a desire to buy a first home, for example, would be very different from those of an older individual saving for retirement or for his or her child's college education.

Individuals and families with limited funds may feel they cannot find someone interested in providing them with financial advice. For many people, their employer is the first place to look for financial advice. Larger companies and many smaller ones provide thrift funds and savings and investment plans to their employees. An employee elects to have a certain sum taken out of his or her paycheck and invested on his or her behalf. In many cases, the employer matches (up to a certain amount) the funds the worker puts in. The individual may choose to have funds placed in a more conservative or higher-risk investment plan. Mutual funds, which by definition include a variety of investments, offer a wide range of investment possibilities depending on one's need for stability or desire for higher returns. Often, a company's human resources department or the administrator of its investment funds can answer any questions that an employee may have.

The Minimum Wage

People earning minimum wage suffer a great deal from inflation, as minimum wage rises only when Congress votes to raise it. Between 1997 and 2007, the federal minimum wage remained at $5.15 an hour. In 2007, Congress agreed to raise it in three stages up to $7.25 an hour. The next increase is likely to be far in the future. Note also, that the $7.25/hr wage does not apply to young workers just starting to work and those who expect a large part of their income in tips (such as waitstaff). In response to inflation, many states have set minimum wages higher than that of the federal government.

Education as a Key to Security and Opportunity

The best way to keep ahead of inflation during one's lifetime is to find employment that offers opportunities for advancement and the flexibility to work in a number of fields. For example, accountants and computer information specialists are needed in manufacturing, banking, energy, and education—indeed, in almost every field imaginable. In today's rapidly evolving markets, it's important not to be tied to only one company or to a shrinking industry.

College students should prepare themselves to work in a number of fields, as the employment market is constantly changing.

Education is becoming more important than ever in finding jobs that will provide job security and salary advancement. University of Chicago finance professor Raghuram Rajan's observations on the growing income inequality in the United States underscore the importance of education. He notes that, since the 1980s, wages of workers (such as office managers) at the 90th percentile of income have grown much faster than those at the 50th percentile. Those at the 50th percentile, the median worker, are typically factory workers and office assistants. According to Rajan, education is the most important factor in this income difference.

Technological advances require a labor force to have better and better skills, requiring more education than was needed in the past. Without more education, middle-class workers will be stuck with job insecurity and flat wages.

The federal government provides a wealth of information about educational opportunities and financing, such as this site hosted by Federal Student Aid (http://www.fafsa.ed.gov).

A report from the Georgetown Center on Education and Workforce that projected jobs and education requirements through 2018 noted that the share of jobs requiring post-secondary education increased from 28 to 59 percent between 1973 and 2008. The same report projected that workers with a high school diploma or less would be limited to only three occupational sectors that are either diminishing in number or offer low wages. They project that such workers will soon be locked out of the middle class due to lack of education.

While education is expensive, it is a worthwhile investment. Another Georgetown Center report, "Education Pays: The Benefits of High Education for Individuals and Society," shows that the higher the level of education, the higher the earnings payoff. The report demonstrates that, in 2002, a bachelor's degree holder could expect to earn 75 percent more over a lifetime than someone with a high school diploma. The difference in lifetime earnings had risen to 84 percent more by 2011.

Such reports indicate that the best investment against inflation is an investment in an education that will result in a lifetime of higher salaries and greater career opportunities. Because almost everyone needs financial aid in order to pay for further education, the U.S. Department of Education provides information about government loans and other educational funding resources for adults as well as young people. The department's Web site also provides links to information about financial literacy and hints on saving for college.

Although the cost of college tuition is rising faster than the general rate of inflation, some states offer programs to pre-pay tuition, enabling the families of future students to lock in tuition at current costs. Keep in mind that reports on greater earnings for those with post-secondary education do not just refer to four-year colleges and universities. There are many lower-priced vocational schools and programs in community colleges that offer certification in numerous fields of study.

Consumer Smarts

Doing research in many areas is important if one hopes to succeed financially in spite of market fluctuations. The motto for stock market investors, "Buy low, sell high," could apply to almost any consumer purchase. However, consumers need to do the math beyond looking at the price of what they intend to buy. Two factors to keep in mind are the cost of buying on credit and the cost of maintenance. For example, if you saved an extra year in order to put down a larger down payment on a clothes washer, how would the savings in interest payments compare to the risk that the price of the item would have gone up in twelve months?

In many cases, people with good credit (meaning they are considered unlikely to default on credit payments) can purchase big-ticket items like home appliances and furniture with a down payment and a year or more "vacation" to pay off the balance interest-free. Of course, there's a catch—payment with interest will come due if the item is not

Financially aware buyers can save money through consumer loyalty programs, buyers' clubs, and store discount cards.

paid for in the agreed-upon amount of time. For those who can take advantage of such offers, this is a great strategy for saving money.

Research on maintenance costs and durability can also help consumers keep ahead of inflation. Many people have discovered that the very cheap printer they bought uses a large amount of very expensive ink. The cheaper refrigerator may cost more in electricity and repairs, and the cheaper vacuum cleaner may have to be replaced after only a year or two. Energy efficiency ratings are posted on new appliances. Consumer ratings on numerous products are available on the Internet and in published reports available at libraries. Thoroughly researching what you plan to buy is a wise investment in time and will result in the saving of money.

Researching the true cost of even small purchases is important, too. Marketers of consumer goods are constantly changing packaging in order to hide rising costs. In the past, items like coffee and bacon were sold in units of 1 pound (0.45 kilograms). Gradually, packages of 12 ounces (340 grams) have become standard, although the packages don't look smaller than the pound sizes. Often, the cost remains the same, despite the fact that there is now a smaller quantity of product. Supermarkets are required to show prices for products in units to help consumers compare prices. Busy shoppers might not take the time to figure out which package or brand is the better bargain, but families and individuals on tight budgets need to pay attention to unit prices. Sadly, it's something that should be monitored from time to time, since companies change packaging often to hide the truth that a smaller amount for the same price means the consumer is paying more.

The Danger of Credit Cards

The spread of credit cards in recent years has made it easy for Americans to spend beyond their means. They may have considered it a hedge against inflation to be able to buy something on credit and benefit from today's price, rather than pay more at tomorrow's price. Young people with no independent income were offered multiple credit cards, which some treated like a magic source of free money. Students left college saddled with student loans and credit card debt at interest rates impossible to pay off by paying only the minimum balance. The Credit Card Act of 2009 addresses these problems by limiting the marketing of credit cards when the students are under twenty-one and requiring an adult to co-sign all applications. This same law requires credit card issuers to make the high cost of this form of consumer credit more apparent.

The need for Congress to step in to protect consumers reminds us that businesses—in this case, banks—are often more focused on profits than on the welfare of their customers. However, it also underscores the need for increased financial literacy in America. Credit card applicants young and old must read the terms of the contract before accepting a card. They should also do the math before charging something they will not be able to pay off fully when the bill comes in. New credit card regulations require card issuers to make interest costs more clear, but they do not provide solutions for those who have charged more than they can handle. Consumers should also study plans like layaway and rent-to-own carefully.

Financial literacy is important for young people. They should learn about the cost of buying on credit to avoid burdensome debt.

Individuals with no credit history have limited financial choices, but they would be wise to explore loans through employer programs and credit unions, and compare the cost of financing their purchases. Establishing a good credit history—a record of paying off debts fully and on time—can save borrowers money for purchases large and small and protect against inflation. This is an essential part of financial literacy that young people should learn early on.

Because Americans have seen their standard of living rise from one generation to the next, most parents expect their children to do better financially than they did. However, the economic turmoil of the first decade of the twenty-first century indicates that Americans cannot assume that their financial futures will be bright. Although wages have risen along with inflation, many hard-working Americans are having trouble financially and can hardly imagine getting ahead.

Even economists cannot predict with certainty the effects of their own efforts to steer the economy in order for it to provide low unemployment, the right amount of economic growth, and the best rate of inflation. A few things are certain however. Education, including financial literacy, is extremely important. Americans should read the small print of contracts before signing and product information before buying, and take the time to calculate the cost of credit. If they do these things, they will already be ahead of the game.

Dig a Little Deeper

To learn more about inflation, do some research to try to answer the following questions:

1. How much will college cost when I am old enough to attend?
2. If inflation continues at the same rate as today, what salary can I expect to earn in various jobs once I begin working?
3. What is the inflation rate today? Is this considered a healthy rate of inflation?
4. Given the current rate of inflation, where is the safest place to put my money? Where will I see the best return on my investment?
5. Are we currently experiencing inflation or deflation?
6. Which is better for an economy, inflation or deflation?
7. When the United States is experiencing inflation, are other countries also experiencing it?
8. When the inflation rate is increasing, is it a good idea to buy things now, when the prices are lower, even if I can't really afford them?
9. My savings account interest rate is 2 percent. The inflation rate is 3.5 percent. Am I losing money by keeping my money in this account?
10. Our house is worth more than it was ten years ago, but our two-year-old car is worth less. Why is this so?

GLOSSARY

asset A resource of economic value owned by a person, company, or country.

bond A debt investment issued by corporations and governments, usually at a fixed rate of interest, to be paid back at a set time.

bubble In economics, a period of extreme and rapid economic expansion, followed by a contraction that may also be extreme and rapid.

credit The purchase of goods or services with agreement to pay later, often over time, and usually with interest.

default The failure of a debtor to make payments on principal and interest when they are due.

deflation A general drop in prices over time, often caused by a reduction of the supply of money or credit.

equity The amount the owner of real estate would receive after selling the property and paying off the mortgage.

exchange rate The value of one currency in relation to another.

fixed Set; unchanging. A fixed rate of interest will stay the same over the life of a loan. People on fixed incomes, such as those receiving Social Security or pensions, get the same amount of money every month.

foreclosure A situation in which a homeowner is unable to make payments on a mortgage, at which point the lender can reclaim the property and sell it to someone else.

hyperinflation A rapid and steep increase in prices of over 50 percent (or more) each month.

inflation A gradual increase in prices over time.

investment A thing that is worth buying because it may be profitable or useful in the future; the act of expending money with the expectation of financial gain.

monetary policy The efforts by a nation's central bank to control economic growth, the rate of inflation, and interest rates by varying the supply of money.

mortgage A long-term loan used to buy real estate, secured by the property it is used to purchase.

mutual fund A type of investment company that raises money from shareholders and invests in a wide range of investments, such as stocks and bonds.

purchasing power The value of currency (like the dollar) expressed in terms of the amount of goods or services that one unit of money can buy.

stagflation A combination of "stagnation" and "inflation," this is a condition of high inflation paired with slow economic growth and high unemployment.

FOR MORE INFORMATION

Bank of Canada
234 Wellington Street
Ottawa, ON K1A 0G9
Canada
(888) 481-1461
Web site: http://www.bankofcanada.ca
This is Canada's central bank with responsibility for setting monetary policy and overseeing currency and financial systems. One of its stated purposes is to preserve the value of money by keeping inflation low and stable.

Federal Deposit Insurance Corporation (FDIC)
3501 North Fairfax Drive
Arlington, VA 22226
(877) ASK-FDIC [275-3342]
Web site: http://www.fdic.gov
The FDIC is an independent agency created by Congress to maintain confidence and stability in the nation's financial system by insuring bank deposits and examining and supervising financial institutions. It is also a source of information for financial literacy and consumer protection.

Federal Reserve
20th Street and Constitution Avenue NW
Washington, DC 20551
(202) 452-3000
Web site: http://www.federalreserve.gov

The Federal Reserve is a system of central banks in the United States. The Board of Governors, based in Washington, D.C., helps set monetary policy. In addition, twelve Reserve Banks around the country act as operating arms to regulate payments, distribute currency, and monitor financial institutions in their geographic regions.

Financial Consumer Agency of Canada
427 Laurier Avenue West, 6th Floor
Ottawa, ON K1R 1B9
Canada
(866) 461-3222
Web site: http://www.fcac-acfc.gc.ca
This agency works to protect and inform consumers of financial products and services in Canada. It provides information to consumers about budgeting and money management, credit, loans, savings, and investments.

U.S. Department of Education
400 Maryland Avenue SW
Washington, DC 20202
(800) USA-LEARN [872-5327]
Web site: http://www.ed.gov
The U.S. Department of Education carries out a number of functions to promote and support education. In relation to financial matters, it provides information and links to resources for everything from financial aid and

education to educational opportunities for the unemployed and financial literacy.

U.S. Department of Labor (DOL)
Frances Perkins Building
200 Constitution Avenue NW
Washington, DC 20210
(877) 889-5927
Web site: http://www.dol.gov
The Department of Labor works to support the needs of American workers, job seekers, and retirees. Within the DOL, the Bureau of Labor Statistics compiles data for the monthly Consumer Price Index, provides an inflation calculator, and keeps track of employment figures.

Web Sites

Due to the changing nature of Internet links, Rosen Publishing has developed an online list of Web sites related to the subject of this book. This site is updated regularly. Please use this link to access the list:

http://www.rosenlinks.com/YEF/Infla

FOR FURTHER READING

Brezina, Corona. *How Deflation Works*. New York, NY: Rosen Publishing, 2010.

Brezina, Corona. *Understanding the Federal Reserve and Monetary Policy*. New York, NY: Rosen Publishing, 2011.

Byers, Ann. *First Credit Cards and Credit Smarts*. New York, NY: Rosen Publishing, 2010.

Chatzky, Jean. *Not Your Parents' Money Book: Making, Saving, and Spending Your Own Money*. New York, NY: Simon & Schuster Books for Young Readers, 2010.

Espejo, Roman, ed. *Teens and Credit*. Farmington Hills, MI: Greenhaven Press, 2010.

Grosz, Ornella. *Moneylicious: A Financial Clue for Generation Y*. Bloomington, IL: Transformation Media Books, 2011.

Hall, Alvin. *Show Me the Money: How to Make Cents of Economics*. New York, NY: DK Publishing, 2008.

Hart, Joyce. *How Inflation Works*. New York, NY: Rosen Publishing, 2009.

Hollander, Barbara G. *How Currency Devaluation Works*. New York, NY: Rosen Publishing, 2011.

Holmberg, Joshua, and David Bruzzese. *The Teen's Guide to Personal Finance: Basic Concepts in Personal Finance That Every Teen Should Know*. Bloomington, IL: iUniverse, 2008.

Howard, Clark. *Clark Howard's Living Large in Lean Times*. New York, NY: Avery, 2011.

Kamberg, Mary-Lane. *Frequently Asked Questions About Financial Literacy.* New York, NY: Rosen Publishing, 2011.

Lanchester, John. *I.O.U.: Why Everyone Owes Everyone and No One Can Pay.* New York, NY: Simon & Shuster, 2010.

Peterson, Judy Monroe. *First Budget Smarts.* New York, NY: Rosen Publishing, 2009.

Poundstone, William. *Priceless: The Myth of Fair Value (and How to Take Advantage of It).* New York, NY: Hill & Wang, 2010.

BIBLIOGRAPHY

Brands, H. W. *Greenback Planet: How the Dollar Conquered the World and Threatened Civilization as We Know It.* Austin, TX: University of Texas Press, 2011.

Carnevale, Anthony P., et al. "The College Payoff: Education, Occupations, Lifetime Earnings." Georgetown University's Center on Education and the Workforce, August 5, 2011. Retrieved March 2012 (http://cew.georgetown.edu/collegepayoff).

Carnevale, Anthony P., et al. "Help Wanted: Projections of Jobs and Education Requirements Through 2018." Georgetown University's Center on Education and the Workforce, June 15, 2010. Retrieved March 2012 (http://cew.georgetown.edu/jobs/2018).

Farnham, Alan. "Three Most Desperate Cities Include Vallejo, Calif., Harrisburg, Pa., Central Falls, R.I." ABC News, September 8, 20ll. Retrieved March 2012 (http://abcnews.go.com/Business).

Fehr, Stephen. "Tracking the Recession: Tuition Programs in Danger." Stateline, April 20, 2009. Retrieved March 2012 (http://www.stateline.org/live/details/story?contentId=393552).

Ferguson, Niall. "Sticker Shock." *Newsweek*, May 9, 2011, p. 8.

InflationData.com. "Misery Index." Retrieved February 2011 (http://inflationdata.com/articles/misery-index).

Lewin, Tamar. "Official Calls for Urgency on College Costs." *New York Times*, November 29, 2011. Retrieved

February 2012 (http://www.nytimes.com/2011/11/30/education/duncan-calls-for-urgency-in-lowering-college-costs.html).

McKenzie, Richard B. *Why Popcorn Costs So Much at the Movies and Other Pricing Puzzles.* New York, NY: Springer Science+Business Media, 2008.

New Jersey League of Municipalities. "State Government and Your Property Taxes." Retrieved February 2012 (http://www.jnslom.org/SG-Property_Taxes.html).

Porter, Eduardo. *The Price of Everything: Solving the Mystery of Why We Pay What We Do.* New York, NY: Portfolio/Penguin, 2011.

Rajan, Raghuram G. *Fault Lines: How Hidden Fractures Still Threaten the World Economy.* Princeton, NJ: Princeton University Press, 2010.

Rickards, James. *Currency Wars: The Making of the Next Global Crisis.* New York, NY: Portfolio/Penguin, 2011.

Rodrik, Dani. *The Globalization Paradox: Democracy and the Future of the World Economy.* New York, NY: W. W. Norton and Company, 2011.

Samuelson, Robert J. *The Great Inflation and Its Aftermath: The Past and Future of American Affluence.* New York, NY: Random House, 2008.

Schwartz, Anna J. "Money Supply." *Concise Encyclopedia of Economics.* Retrieved February 2012 (http://www.econlib.org//library/Enc/MoneySupply.html).

Sowell, Thomas. *Basic Economics. A Common Sense Guide to the Economy.* 4th ed. New York, NY: Basic Books, 2011.

Sowell, Thomas. *The Housing Boom and Bust.* New York, NY: Basic Books, 2009.

Stiglitz, Joseph E. *Freefall: America, Free Markets, and the Sinking of the World Economy.* New York, NY: W. W. Norton and Company, 2010.

Wessel, David. *In Fed We Trust: Ben Bernanke's War on the Great Panic.* New York, NY: Crown Publishing, 2009.

INDEX

P

R

S

U

V

About the Author

Writer and educator Terry Teague Meyer, Ph.D., has professional experience in the fields of education, energy, and municipal administration. She served for many years on the board of directors of a municipal utility district in the Houston area. She has lived long enough to observe and experience the effects of inflation. While researching this book, she gained a greater understanding of the government's role in steering the economy.

Photo Credits

Cover (bottom) © iStockphoto.com/Don Bayley; cover (torn paper) © iStockphoto.com/Petek Arici; pp. 4, 14 Scott Olson/Getty Images; pp. 7, 18, 28, 37, 53 © iStockphoto .com/Ivan Bliznetsov; p. 8 Michael Nagle/Getty Images; pp. 10–11, 19, 32–33, 34, 44–45, 50–51, 58–59 © AP Images; pp. 16–17, 38–39 David McNew/Getty Images; p. 21 Universal Images Group/Getty Images; p. 24 Mario Tama/Getty Images; p. 26 MCT/Getty Images; pp. 29, 48 Justin Sullivan/Getty Images; p. 30 ChinaFotoPress/ Getty Images; pp. 40–41 Spencer Platt/Getty Images; pp. 54–55 Eric Audras/PhotoAlto Agency/Getty Images; p. 62 Hemera/Thinkstock; p. 65 Jupiterimages/Brand X Pictures/Thinkstock.

Designer: Michael Moy; Photo Researcher: Amy Feinberg